MORE THAN Just a HAIRDRESSER Workbook

The ability to live
a fulfilled
and peaceful life
IS POSSIBLE
and completely
within your grasp.

DONNA PIROMALLI

Donna Piromalli
Books & Coaching Programs

Books
More Than Just a Hairdresser - Book
More Than Just a Hairdresser - Workbook
The Art of Gratitude - Journal

Programs

THE ART OF LIVING PROGRAM
An individual program tailored to your specific needs for personal or professional growth or both.

THE ART OF POSITIVE CULTURE
An "in salon" program to address the needs of the business and group dynamics of the salon environment.

For More Information
Please Visit
www.DonnaPiromalli.com
www.griffithcounselling.com

Copyright © 2020 by Donna Piromalli

All rights reserved. This book may not be reproduced in whole or in part, by any means, without the written consent of the publisher. For permission requests, write to the publisher, addressed "Attention Permissions Coordinator" at the address below.

Donna Piromalli
P.O. BOX 1152
Griffith, NSW 2680
Australia

More Than "Just a Hairdresser"

I would like a change, but not too much off my length,
Because in biblical times, my hair gave me strength.
This strength to be a woman, and show I am much more,
I love my luscious locks, for they inspire me to soar.

I can be myself and feel comfort in my own skin,
If you change me too quickly, I may never be 'me' again.
I am open to ideas and love the creativity you show,
You are a vital part of my journey through life as I grow.

You make me feel safe, as your fingers run through my hair,
You are a confidant, a friend, I know you really care.
You are there at life's occasions, and plan them with me,
From weddings to funerals, almost closer than family.

When the sad times arrive, and fragility affects my condition,
You arrive with turbans and wigs, soothing tears like a magician.
You are more than just a hairdresser, how much you may never know,
You bring me joy, confidence and sooth my very soul!

Donna Piromalli

Make Over Your Mindset!

This workbook is designed as a companion guide to my book, *More Than Just a Hairdresser*. I created the workbook to help guide you through making some decisions about who you are and what you want out of your life.

It is true that you may frequently hear or read about changing certain things in your life. While you may be excited at the time, it is easy to slide back into the routine of life without pursuing those ideas and dreams. I have found through my years of guiding clients toward their best life, that writing down what you want, and then taking action, is the only way to really accomplish your goals.

You will be guided through the pages of this workbook to discover who you really are as a person and what is important to you right now. Part of that discovery involves imagining your future and then developing a path to achieve those dreams.

When I started implementing growth and change in my own life years ago, I could have never imagined how far it would take me. But imagining that ultimate life is not the point of this workbook. The point is to imagine the next few years, the next few steps, the first part of the path.

If you were to stand back and look at a huge mountain, it will seem overwhelming to climb it all at once. But if you first learn information about the mountain, and then implement small steps every day, you will find that you reach the summit quite quickly, and with much less effort, than you might have guessed when you first gazed upon that far off peak.

Life is the same as that mountain. You begin with the first few steps to get you started on your own journey of 'becoming'. While part of that will include learning about those around you, it will also include a great deal of understanding about yourself.

Contents

Section 1
A New Do
7

Section 2
Layering Your Life
23

Section 3
Deep Conditioning Treatment
41

Section 4
The Economy of Style
55

Section 5
Salon Life 101
77

Section 6
Taming Life's Split Ends
101

I think it is possible for ordinary people to choose to be extraordinary.

Elon Musk

Section 1

A New Do

Section 1
A New Do

The basis for my book "More Than Just a Hairdresser" is to provide a tool for you to examine your life and then create a plan to make the changes you desire. Without a doubt, in order to change anything, you must first decide what it is that you want. This is a necessary first step to create your own unique road map to a better life.

To begin, I'm going to take you through a few exercises. I want you to realise that there are no right or wrong answers, you will just be dreaming about your future life and examining your current life. I would caution you not to fall into the trap of self-editing your ideas and dreams. Often, a dream or goal will pop into our heads, only to have the logical side of our mind convince us that its "not possible" or "not practical". You must understand that your logical mind builds those boundaries based on the past, not the future. Therefore, there are no real limitations on what can be if you allow it.

There are numerous exercises that follow that will require you to specifically write down what you want. I would encourage you to create those statements in the most positive way you can imagine. For example, instead of saying, "I want to not get involved in personal drama at the salon," you might say, "I will stay professional and above any drama at the salon." This states what you do want rather than what you don't want, which is very important.

By making those statements positive and certain, you are telling your mind that they will happen. You are making a commitment to change, and that commitment is vital to accomplishing the goals you set later on in this workbook. You are also not expressing those ideas as a dream or wish. By saying things like "I want to" or "I hope to" instead of "I will" you are allowing yourself an out to fail before you even get started. This is why things like New Years' resolutions rarely work. They are stated as a wish or hope rather than as a solid commitment to yourself with a plan to back it up.

My Dreams and Ideas

Write down what you really want no matter how outrageous or impractical it may seem today. Dream as if time and money were no object. Dream as if you aren't weighted down with responsibilities and to do lists. Dream as if anything is possible.

Imagine your life in five years. Where do you want to live? What will you enjoy? What kind of lifestyle? Be specific. Picture that life in your mind and describe everything you see.

_____
_____
_____
_____
_____
_____
_____
_____
_____
_____
_____
_____
_____
_____
_____
_____
_____
_____

Imagine your life ten years from now. Describe it in detail. What will you have accomplished? What will your family or personal life be like? How will your business have changed or grown?

This next step may take a bit more time. We all have faults and things we don't necessarily do well right now, but those habits and thought processes can be changed over time. This workbook is all about your journey to 'becoming' that person you want to be.

When you think about yourself, and the person you are right now, today, how do you imagine that you will change as a person over the next ten years? What kind of person do you want to become in that time frame?

_____
_____
_____
_____
_____
_____
_____
_____
_____
_____
_____
_____
_____
_____
_____
_____
_____

Describe how you will change in detail. How will you treat people? What will you have learned about yourself and others?

Now think about some things you are currently struggling with. This includes events from your past, current relationships, or other problems you deal with frequently.

What personal issues will you have overcome ten years from now?

_____
_____
_____
_____
_____
_____
_____
_____
_____
_____
_____
_____
_____
_____
_____
_____
_____
_____
_____
_____

How will these issues change and how will your life have improved because of that change?

_____
_____
_____
_____
_____
_____
_____
_____
_____
_____
_____
_____
_____
_____
_____
_____
_____
_____
_____
_____
_____
_____
_____

What kind of partner/parent/friend do you want to be to those in your life?

Describe those relationships and what you envision them becoming.

What professional milestones do you want to have accomplished or perfected? List these.

What kind of professional do you imagine becoming? What will your skillset be? How will you relate to clients each day?

When clients think of you, what impression do you want them to have of who you have become?

These initial steps are designed to get you in the frame of mind to really dig deep into the future you. The you that you really want to become. This is how we discover our own personal vision. No one can tell you what your vision should be for your life, but as you go back and review what you wrote for the steps you just completed, it will become clear what vision you have for your life.

So often, when I ask what someone wants from life they will say something like, "I want to be successful" or "I want to be happy." But what do those words really mean? Success and happiness aren't a point you arrive at and the idea of what those words mean is different for each of us. Now I want you to define each of those words for yourself and be specific. Describe what it looks like in your future life.

In my life, the word 'success' means:

_____
_____
_____
_____
_____
_____
_____
_____
_____
_____
_____
_____
_____
_____
_____

When I think of the word 'happiness', to me it means:

As you change and grow, your idea of both success and happiness will change, and it should. We each grow and develop at our own pace and that change produces more change. You can think of it like a snowball. Once you start rolling, the growth accelerates.

It is easy to look at someone who is farther along the path and think you have no chance to achieve something similar. But it's not true. You are just as capable, but you must make the decision to choose growth over stagnation. I often say that what you focus on expands and that is true in the area of personal growth. Once you start to change, your confidence in yourself expands exponentially; beyond what you can even imagine right now, but that will never happen if you don't start.

This is your opportunity to harness that power by gaining clarity of vision for your life and then implementing a plan to make that vision a reality.

The only place where success comes before work is in the dictionary.

Vidal Sassoon

*The most difficult thing is the decision to act.
The rest is merely tenacity.*

Amelia Earhart

Section 2

Layering Your Life

Section 2
Layering Your Life

Nothing that comes easy is worthwhile. I know you have probably heard that said many times and may even believe it whole heartedly. The only problem with that idea is that we assume what we want is too hard to achieve, so we don't even start. That life you just dreamed about in the previous section, may seem almost impossible from where you sit right now and that can be discouraging.

I am here to show you how to make those dreams a reality and it doesn't happen by trying to climb the whole mountain in one day. As I said in my book, the solution is taking one step at a time even if you don't know all the steps. Forward motion creates more forward motion and as the first step or two is accomplished, the next step becomes obvious.

Achieving anything takes consistent and ongoing effort. Many people don't even start on the path because the goals they dream of seem so out of reach. Others start but are inconsistent and eventually they let their dreams fall by the wayside. None of these issues has to do with the fact that they can't achieve their goals. It has to do with their level of personal commitment to that goal and their ability to stay consistent in working toward achieving it.

Your time is limited, so don't waste it living someone else's life.

Steve Jobs

A Goal Without a Plan is Just a Wish

I talk about goal setting a lot in my coaching and counselling practice. Goal setting is one of the areas that it seems everyone knows about, and knows they should do, but few really understand how to set up their goals into action steps to achieve anything. Many people also feel that they just can't add one more thing to their lives. They are pulled in so many different directions every day and feel as if they don't have time to do everything now, let alone add some lofty goals to the mix.

However, accomplishing more does not have anything to do with magically creating more time. It has to do with organising what you are doing now and prioritising what you really want. You don't have to create more time. You have exactly the same amount of time each day as those who are self-made billionaires. The only difference is in how that time is managed and how committed you are to achieving the life you want. To start this goal setting exercise, look back at the last section and review those dreams.

Now I want you to make a list of 20 things that you want to accomplish in the next five years. This includes professionally, personally, and in every other area you can think of. Make the full list and don't quit until you get to 20.

Step 1: Goals to reach the next five years

1. _____
2. _____
3. _____
4. _____
5. _____
6. _____
7. _____
8. _____
9. _____
10. _____
11. _____
12. _____
13. _____
14. _____
15. _____
16. _____
17. _____
18. _____
19. _____
20. _____

Look at that list and really think about it. Did you leave anything out? If so, go back and add it now. Once you feel your list is complete, move on to the next step.

Now you will go through and number your list 1-20 by how important you feel that goal is - the most important goal should be #1 and the least important #20. Don't think about which goal is the easiest to reach or the most practical! Think about the one that you connect with on an emotional level and want so very much, even if it seems the hardest to achieve. Once you have them numbered rewrite the list in order here.

Step 2: Prioritise the list

1. _____
2. _____
3. _____
4. _____
5. _____
6. _____
7. _____
8. _____
9. _____
10. _____
11. _____
12. _____
13. _____
14. _____
15. _____
16. _____
17. _____
18. _____
19. _____
20. _____

Now that you have the list prioritised, this is your long-term goal list. These long-term goals may change over time, but they will be your guiding direction for the next few years.

You will now take these long-term goals and focus on the top ten. These are the ones you really want. The other goals are also important, but these ten must come first when you think about taking action!

Now for each of these ten goals, you are going to list the action steps you will need to take over the next two years to begin the process of achieving them. The easiest way to show you how to do this is with an example. Let's say your #1 long term goal is to achieve financial independence so you can choose how hard to work, or whether to work at all, in the future.

To start the process, we will take that goal of financial independence and list three smaller short-term goals. These are what you will work on the next 12-24 months. Your list might look like this:

Long Term Goal #1 – Achieve Financial Independence

Short term goals:
- A. Lower all basic expenses by at least 20%.
- B. Pay off $4,000 in high interest debt.
- C. Establish an emergency fund of $10,000.

Now as you can see, these are pretty basic goals but as the saying goes, though they be small, they be mighty! Now that you have these short-term goals, you take each one and define immediate action steps, this is Step 3.

Step 3: Daily Action Steps

Daily action steps for each short term goal should be short, easy to accomplish steps you can take weekly or daily depending on the goal.

For example, for short term goal A, Lower all basic expenses, you might list the following:

    a. Review all bank statements for monthly subscriptions or expenses I'm not using and cancel them.
    b. Find a cheaper place to live or see about taking on a roommate.
    c. Cut eating out by 1/3 this month and cook at home.

This is a very simplified list and it focuses on things you can do each day to accomplish that first short term goal that will allow you to make progress toward the long term goal. This one is quite easy, but let's take one that seems harder, like short term goal C, the $10,000 emergency fund.

For many people saving that kind of money seems near impossible! But is it really? Again, let's take the idea and break it down into small steps. Let's assume you want to save this amount all in one year – an even loftier goal. In one year, assuming you work five days per week, you have approximately 250 working days (this includes taking at least two weeks to go on holiday). At that rate if you want to save $10,000 in one year you will need to save $200 per week, or $40 per working day.

Now think about that, if you are already working toward lowering your expenses and paying off your debt, then $40 per day seems much more doable because you will be freeing up additional money you already bring in. What if you also worked an extra hour each day or a couple of weekends per month? If you put that money back as well, you could easily have $10,000 in one year depending on your salary level.

The average hairdresser in Australia makes a little more than $20 per hour. If you make less, then it might take you two years instead of one, but it is still very achievable if you are committed to the goal every day and put back the money as you earn it.

What if you worked two extra days each month? That would accomplish the same goal so there are numerous options to make the math work once you realise how much you need to put back each week.

The point is, that what may have seemed a huge goal, when broken down into daily action steps suddenly becomes something you can achieve — but only if you are committed to it and willing to change your habits.

In the next few pages, I want you to take the first ten goals on your list and break each one down in short term goals and then daily action steps.

Goal Setting Worksheet

#1_____

    A._____

        a._____

        b._____

        c._____

    B._____

        a._____

        b._____

        c._____

    C._____

        a._____

        b._____

        c._____

#2 _____

    A. _____

        a. _____

        b. _____

        c. _____

    B. _____

        a. _____

        b. _____

        c. _____

    C. _____

        a. _____

        b. _____

        c. _____

#3 _____

    A. _____

        a. _____

        b. _____

        c. _____

    B. _____

        a. _____

        b. _____

        c. _____

    C. _____

        a. _____

        b. _____

        c. _____

#4_____

    A._____

        a._____

        b._____

        c._____

    B._____

        a._____

        b._____

        c._____

    C._____

        a._____

        b._____

        c._____

#5_____

    A._____

        a._____

        b._____

        c._____

    B._____

        a._____

        b._____

        c._____

    C._____

        a._____

        b._____

        c._____

You will do this same thing for the rest of your top twenty goals as well. The main thing this exercise does is help you realise you can help yourself achieve what you want in very small ways each and every day. But not if you don't think about those steps and review them each day.

This is why so many fail to achieve what they say they want. Once they dream the big goal, they stop. They never create a stepping path of smaller goals and they never set themselves daily tasks to make sure it happens. They just dream the big dream and a year later are still dreaming.

While this may seem a little tedious at first, it allows you to create a path to follow. You are doing the hard work up front so you will be able to be consistent over the course of a year. As you accomplish each of the smaller goals, set new ones that get you even closer to that long-term dream. Over time, and probably much faster than you can imagine, you will achieve those 20 long term goals and be able to set new, higher ones.

As you move through this process, I want to encourage you to track your progress. Write down what happens as you work toward your goals. It is human nature to diminish our accomplishments and focus on our failures. Check off on your list when you accomplish that step and put a date!

Track your progress and keep a journal of all the things you do each week that get you closer to reaching those goals. There are few things more life affirming, than to look back over the course of a year or two and see how far you have come. It forces you to recognise your own innate power to accomplish the things you want. It also gives you the encouragement to keep going which is so very important.

I have clients who have keep journals for literally decades. They love going back and seeing where they were in their personal growth at age 25, 30, 40, even 50. No one will be more amazed than you years from now at how far you were able to come and all the accomplishments and accolades you will have received. But it will only happen if you plan for it. Set those goals now and take action every day.

Focus on YOU

As I talked about in the book, when you think of changing your life, it is important to focus on only those things that you can control. I used this Circle of Control illustration to show exactly what your sphere of control encompasses. Ask yourself, what is inside my control right now and what is outside my control?

I am not a product of my circumstances. I am a product of my decisions.

Stephen Covey

When you set your goals, you must focus on steps you can accomplish, not worry about things outside your control. These goals are meant to improve your own life and there is little you can do about others' actions or events that happened in the past. I realise that while this is easy to say, it is often hard to implement.

You may spend a great deal of time worrying or being angry over something that is completely out of your control. However, no amount of concern or anger about something out of your control will fix the issue or change things. You must instead focus on the areas that you have control over and let the rest go. Accomplishing something, anything, toward your goals relieves a great deal of worry and anxiety about those things you can do nothing about.

Do you want to look back a year from now and realise you spent hours, days, or weeks agonizing over a situation that you could do nothing about? How will you feel when you realise that time could have been spent working toward one of your life goals? Think about that now and stop those emotions from taking time away from your daily goal tasks.

As you look at the tasks you really want to accomplish, think about those things in your life that right now take up a great deal of time. It will help if you pick a typical week and track what you do during all of your waking hours. Now answer the following questions:

How much time do you spend in the car getting from point A to point B?

___

How much time at work do you spend actually working versus doing other tasks?

___

How much 'down' time do you have during the day that you currently aren't using that could be time spent reaching your goals?

_____
_____
_____
_____
_____
_____
_____
_____

How many tasks can you combine, delegate or eliminate?

_____
_____
_____
_____
_____
_____
_____
_____
_____
_____
_____

Look back at the typical daily task list that you just created by tracking your waking hours and do some evaluation. Some of these tasks may take only a few minutes out of your day but over time, they add up.

Now ask yourself: Can you do them while you are waiting to pick up your children from school or classes? Can you free up some time by combining tasks/errands? Perhaps instead of going to buy groceries a couple times each week, you go once each week or once every other week.

List several ways you will consolidate these tasks this week/month:

_____
_____
_____
_____
_____
_____
_____
_____
_____
_____
_____
_____
_____
_____
_____
_____

Not only does this keep your expenses better under control because you are thinking about your purchases instead of impulse buying, it also frees up a great deal of time. Are there tasks like laundry or housework that can be delegated to children or other household members?

List the tasks you will delegate to others:

_____
_____
_____
_____
_____
_____
_____
_____
_____
_____
_____
_____
_____

Almost every single person can completely eliminate at least 10% or more of the things they do now that don't serve their goals. By also combining tasks and delegating you can easily free up another 10%-15%.

If you had 25% more time every day to focus on the goals you really want, how much further along would you be a year from now? This is completely within your control, you just have to recognise the benefit and put these ideas in place.

The art of living lies less in eliminating our troubles than growing with them

Bernard M. Baruch

Section 3

Deep Conditioning Treatment

Section 3
Deep Conditioning Treatment

One of the best ways you can help yourself achieve more is to really get to know who you are right now. Not the person you'd like to think you are, but the real you. Within my book I talk a lot about the conscious and subconscious mind. They are extremely powerful and understanding how they work together either for or against your new goals is important.

As I noted in my book, this stick figure has been around about 100 years and was originally developed as an illustration by Dr. Thurman Fleet. The reason it has had such a powerful impact all those years is because it is such a simple representation of how our minds work.

Everything we know or learn is taken in through our senses into the conscious mind. Those experiences and ideas are stored in our subconscious and over time, they develop into how we view the world. While the ideas in our subconscious mind aren't set in stone, they can be tough to overcome. However, your determination to change is the key factor in revising your current view of the world.

I want to remind you in this section how this works because you are going to be taking a test that will show the key factors in your personality. These factors will include your strengths and weaknesses as well as show how you respond to stress or frustration.

When you really start to understand your normal tendencies, you can put in the effort to capitalise on what you do well while at the same time work on those issues that are holding you back.

Personality Test

There are many personality tests in existence today. This is a very simplified version of some of those and will give you a quick overview of your own personality. This is important because once you understand the basic makeup of the various personalities it will help you manage change within yourself. It will also help you reduce conflict and work better with the other people in your life right now.

Please remember that there are no wrong answers here. The younger a person is, the more likely they will have one main personality type. However, as we age, we tend to take on some of the positive qualities of other personalities as well.

This is natural because we mature and learn the value of working well with other people. This allows us to suppress the negative qualities of our main personality type but also take on the more positive qualities of others. By taking this type of test, it focuses your attention on how you can improve over time and allows you to achieve a balanced, less emotional response to stress in your life.

Instructions:
In the following test, there are ten lines containing four sets of words. For each line of four words, rank them in order of which word describes you best (4) to which describes you least (1) in each line.

A	B	C	D
1. __ Likes Authority	__ Enthusiastic	__ Sensitive Feelings	__ Likes Instructions
2. __ Takes Charge	__ Takes Risks	__ Loyal	__ Accurate
3. __ Determined	__ Visionary	__ Calm, Even Keel	__ Consistent
4. __ Enterprising	__ Very Verbal	__ Enjoys Routine	__ Predictable
5. __ Competitive	__ Promoter	__ Dislikes Change	__ Practical
6. __ Problem Solver	__ Enjoys Popularity	__ Gives In To Others	__ Factual
7. __ Productive	__ Fun-Loving	__ Avoids Confrontations	__ Conscientious
8. __ Bold	__ Likes Variety	__ Sympathetic	__ Perfectionist
9. __ Decision Maker	__ Spontaneous	__ Nurturing	__ Detail-Oriented
10. __ Persistent	__ Inspirational	__ Peacemaker	__ Analytical

Now add the numbers for each column below:

TOTAL "A" _____   TOTAL "B" _____   TOTAL "C" _____   TOTAL "D" _____

Who You Are

Remember this is just a very general test and a quick snapshot of who you are right now. It's not uncommon to be a combination of types and this will change over time. As you read through these descriptions, think about your own personality and how you react to conflict. Then take a minute and think about people in your personal and work life. Can you spot some of their personalities as well?

A – DeeAnn Dominant

This personality type is a leader and often are bosses, managers or entrepreneurs. They are confident, decisive and love to solve problems. This confidence can mean they tend to run over the feelings of others or take charge immediately if there is a need. Their assertiveness is often interpreted as aggression and this can lead to conflict. People with this personality tend to be very strongly this type with much less of the other personalities mixed in.

Personality Strengths

- Goal-oriented
- Achievement driven
- Gets results
- Independent
- Risk-taker
- Takes initiative
- Self-starter
- Persistent

Personality Weaknesses

- Blunt
- Poor listener
- Impulsive
- Demanding
- May put projects over people
- May "run over" others who hesitate/think first
- Fears inactivity, relaxation
- Quickly bored by routine or mechanics

Overall Attributes: This personality is motivated by results and action. They like to get credit for the things they have done. They like freedom, authority and thrive in an environment with difficult assignments and opportunity for advancement. They tend to make quick decisions with few facts necessary.

When in Conflict: This personality can become very autocratic and tends to not listen to others when conflict arises. They will often try to assert more control in a difficult situation and can become frustrated if a solution to issues isn't found quickly.

B - Sally Social

This personality is great fun. They are enthusiastic and tend to be cheerleader types. They are often in positions that require meeting new people constantly, like sales or marketing. They are fabulous networkers and love connecting people. They have extensive verbal skills and seem to get along with most everyone. They love attention and have a strong desire to be liked. Often, they are the fashionista of the workplace and take great care in their appearance.

Personality Strengths

- Enthusiastic
- Optimistic
- Good Communicator
- Emotional and Passionate
- Motivational and Inspirational
- Outgoing
- Personal
- Dramatic
- Good Ideas

Personality Weaknesses

- Unrealistic
- Not detail-oriented
- Disorganised
- Impulsive
- Listens to feelings above logic
- Reactive
- Can be too talkative
- Excitable
- Little follow though

Overall attributes: This personality is fun loving, and people oriented. They focus on the future and tend to run from project to project. They can inspire and encourage others and like a team environment. They make very good intuitive decisions.

When in Conflict: This personality can be verbally vicious and talk in a derogatory manner about others when in conflict. When angry, they can make rash decisions that are very detrimental to themselves and others long term. They often put being liked above making good decisions. Other personalities can view Sally Social as two faced when in conflict.

C – Patty Passive

This personality is very loyal and consequently will put up with a lot of emotional pain in a given situation. They tend to stay in one job or with one employer for long periods of time and are people pleasers. They want everyone to get along and don't want to rock the boat. This personality can be found in a profession that will allow them to stay in the background.

Personality Strengths

- Patient
- Easy-going
- Team player
- Stable
- Empathetic
- Compassionate
- Tremendously loyal
- Puts people above projects
- Dependable, Reliable, Agreeable

Personality Weaknesses

- Indecisive
- Over-accommodating
- May sacrifice results for the sake of harmony
- Slow to initiate
- Avoids confrontation even when needed
- Tends to hold grudges and remember hurts
- May refuse to see facts or issues
- Can have problems with pacing or production
- Seen as a follower/few original ideas

Overall Attributes: This personality is extremely loyal, works at a relaxed pace and is very people oriented. They focus on having good relationships even if it means their needs or desires are set aside. They are wonderful listeners and communicators and like a long-term consistent environment. They make decisions slowly and require a lot of information to do so.

When in Conflict: This personality can often shut down in order to avoid more conflict. They suppress their own wants and needs and can become very unhappy. They don't adjust well to change and can be very resistant. They will tend to talk about others rather than address conflict in a straightforward way.

D - Nancy Nitpicky

This personality has a strong need to do things correctly and tend to be rule followers. They read and follow instructions very well and can be found frequently in professions that require accuracy, like accounting, or that require adherence to rules, like law. They tend to have extremely high standards of both themselves and others and can get frustrated with others who they feel don't live up to their standards. Because of this tendency to put rules over people, they can often come across as cold or heartless.

Personality Strengths

- Accurate
- Analytical
- Detail-oriented
- Thoroughness
- Industrious
- Orderly
- Methodical and exhaustive
- High standards, very controlled

Personality Weaknesses

- Too hard on self
- Too critical of others
- Perfectionist
- Overly cautious
- Won't make decisions without "all" the facts
- Too picky
- Overly sensitive
- Can stall or halt progress

Overall Attributes: This personality is very task oriented and thorough. They are focused on high standards and quality and tend to be slow paced valuing quality over speed. They are usually diplomatic and good listeners. They require a tremendous amount of information to make a decision and will often avoid decisions completely. They prefer gradual change and clearly defined tasks and expectations.

When in Conflict: This personality will absolutely avoid conflict at all costs. They will ignore deadlines and prefer to do things themselves as opposed to involving others. They tend to be loners and are naturally skeptical. They will not share a lot of personal details. They are not risk takers and become very passive aggressive if pushed.

Improving Communication

I often use this type of personality information when I counsel couples and families. It is not uncommon for opposites to attract so you will frequently have partners with completely opposite personalities. This is not bad, it just takes understanding how to communicate effectively with that specific personality type and what aspects of your personality that might make communication more challenging.

As you can imagine after reading the basic personality types, how they each approach and deal with conflict is critical to understand. By knowing what that personality needs to make a decision, embrace change, or overcome an obstacle it allows you to find ways to meet those needs and find common ground.

For example, if you know your partner or coworker is a Nancy Nitpicky personality and you need them to make a decision, you know they will need tremendous amounts of research or information to get comfortable with that idea. You also will know they are slow paced and need time. This means that if you are a DeeAnn Dominate, you will have to hold back on your natural frustration with indecision and not run over them to make a quick decision as that will lead to more conflict.

It is through this type of understanding of your own personality, and theirs, that you can start to make great progress toward improving the various relationships in your life. That in turn leads to balance and peace. No one wants constant conflict and reducing that conflict in every area adds to your overall long-term happiness.

Life is 10 percent what happens to me and 90 percent of how I react to it.

Charles Swindoll

Some clients I work with will say they have no conflict in their lives but have to deal with angry coworkers all the time. It is important to understand that conflict manifests itself in the form of anger frequently. One visual I use to illustrate this is the Anger Iceberg. Anger is just like this iceberg because the emotion or behaviors we see is only a small part of what is really going on beneath the surface.

Anger is usually a result of many other emotions from frustration to embarrassment. It is important to understand this because if you just focus on the anger, it escalates. However, if you seek to understand the person you are in conflict with, the real emotion behind that anger can be discovered. That is what I help my clients do every day. Uncover the root of the conflict so it can be dealt with in an effective manner.

Think about the last time you were angry with someone in your life or someone was angry with you. Explain what happened:

_____
_____
_____
_____
_____
_____
_____
_____
_____
_____
_____
_____
_____
_____
_____
_____
_____
_____
_____
_____
_____
_____
_____
_____
_____

Now think about your personality, and theirs. What do you believe was the real emotion behind that anger?

What specific personality traits (yours and theirs) may have increased that conflict?

How might you resolve that conflict differently with what you have learned so far in this workbook?

Your Choices Determine Your Outcome

Success is the sum of small efforts, repeated day in and day out.

Robert Collier

Section 4

The Economy of Style

Section 4
The Economy of Style

Part of deciding what you want out of life and setting goals to get there, is the realisation that you must also care for yourself. We have all over-committed to various things in our lives at times. Though you want to spend time achieving your goals, you must also ensure that your life does not become completely unbalanced over a long stretch of time.

While there are periods in your life that one area or the other may need to take priority, you can't have an unbalanced life for an extended period of time otherwise you will become exhausted and unhappy. In my book, I discussed the illustration on the next page.

If you look at what you have in life, you'll always have more. If you look at what you don't have in life, you'll never have enough.

Oprah Winfrey

The Wheel of Life

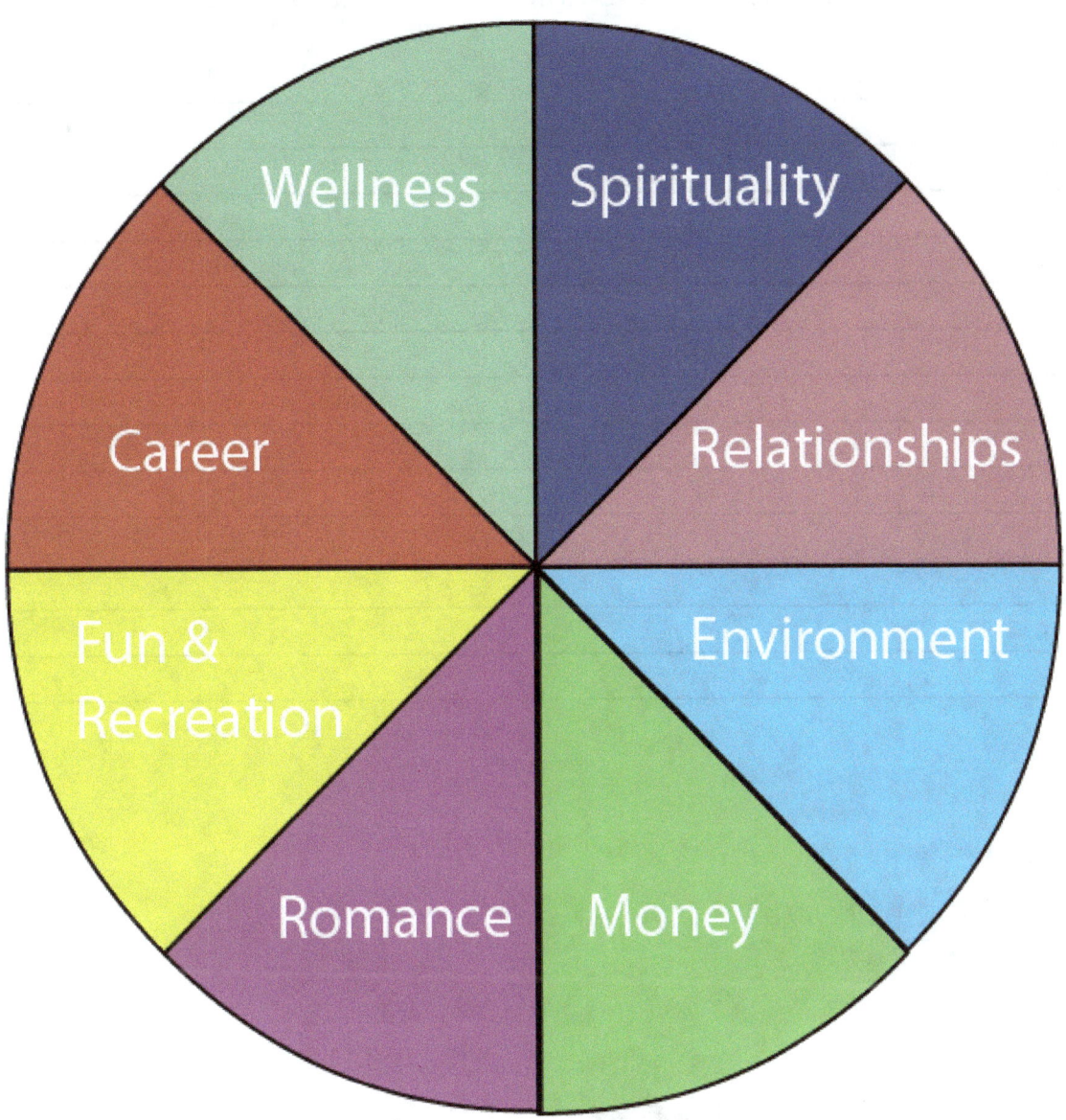

Attention to each of these areas is vital to feel fulfilled and happy. In this section I will be asking you a lot of questions about each area. Be honest, even if at this moment you aren't paying much attention to a particular area. These questions are designed for you to recognise your own needs as a human being and think about how to meet those needs. It is very easy to get in the habit of putting your own needs last. I teach my clients that only through self-care on a consistent basis will you be able to be there emotionally for those in your life. You can't do that if you are mentally exhausted all the time or feel stretched too thin.

Money

How do you feel about where you are right now financially?

_____
_____
_____
_____
_____
_____
_____
_____
_____
_____
_____
_____
_____

What do you feel you have done well so far regarding your finances?

_____
_____
_____
_____
_____
_____
_____
_____
_____
_____
_____
_____
_____
_____
_____

How do you feel you can improve your financial situation?

_____
_____
_____
_____
_____
_____
_____
_____
_____
_____
_____
_____
_____
_____
_____

Romance

Describe your current/most recent romantic relationship.

_____
_____
_____
_____
_____
_____
_____
_____
_____
_____
_____
_____
_____

What do/did you find fulfilling about that romantic relationship?

_____
_____
_____
_____
_____
_____
_____
_____
_____
_____
_____
_____
_____
_____

What do you feel you can do to make your current relationship better or to find a good romantic relationship in the future?

_____
_____
_____
_____
_____
_____
_____
_____
_____
_____
_____
_____
_____
_____
_____
_____

Environment

How do you feel about where you live and work?

_____
_____
_____
_____
_____
_____
_____
_____
_____
_____
_____
_____
_____

What are the good aspects of your current environment?

How do you feel you can improve your current home and work environment?

Fun & Recreation

When was the last time you did something fun that you really enjoyed? Describe it:

_____
_____
_____
_____
_____
_____
_____
_____
_____
_____
_____
_____
_____

How often do you do things with friends/family that allow you to have fun?

_____
_____
_____
_____
_____
_____
_____
_____
_____
_____
_____
_____
_____
_____
_____

What are some ideas for fun or recreational activities that you would like to add to your life?

_____
_____
_____
_____
_____
_____
_____
_____
_____
_____
_____
_____
_____

Career

How do you feel about your career right now?

_____
_____
_____
_____
_____
_____
_____
_____
_____
_____
_____
_____
_____
_____

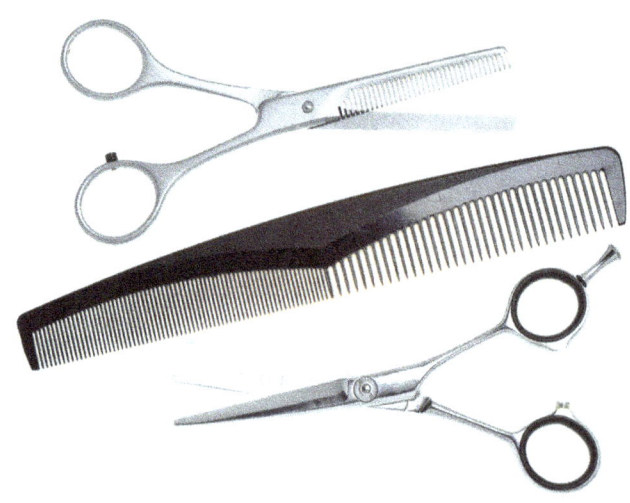

Name three things that are positive about your career or that you do especially well.

_____
_____
_____
_____
_____
_____
_____
_____
_____
_____
_____
_____
_____
_____

List three things that you would like to focus on/change in your career.

_____
_____
_____
_____
_____
_____
_____
_____
_____
_____
_____
_____
_____
_____

Relationships

What relationships do you have personally or professionally that you feel add positively to your life?

_____
_____
_____
_____
_____
_____
_____
_____
_____
_____
_____
_____
_____
_____
_____
_____
_____
_____

What is it about those relationships that you want to keep/replicate in other relationships?

_____
_____
_____
_____
_____
_____
_____
_____
_____
_____
_____
_____
_____

List the relationships in your life that you feel need work and what you'd like to see changed.

_____
_____
_____
_____
_____
_____
_____
_____
_____
_____
_____
_____
_____
_____
_____

Wellness

How do you feel about your overall health both physically and mentally right now?

_____
_____
_____
_____
_____
_____
_____
_____
_____
_____
_____
_____
_____
_____

What parts of your physical or mental health do you feel are good and why?

_____
_____
_____
_____
_____
_____
_____
_____
_____
_____
_____
_____
_____
_____

What areas of your health, either physically or mentally, would you like to improve?

_____
_____
_____
_____
_____
_____
_____
_____
_____
_____
_____
_____
_____
_____

Spirituality

What activities in your life right now give you inspiration or make you feel positive and hopeful?

_____
_____
_____
_____
_____
_____
_____
_____
_____
_____
_____
_____
_____
_____
_____

What events or activities do you feel you can add to your life that will help you feel uplifted and happy?

___

Think back on the times when you felt inspired and energised to take action? What spurred that inspiration? How can you incorporate something similar in your life today?

___

The most important take away from this section of the workbook is the understanding that you are in control of each of these areas. How big a role they play in your daily life is up to you, but each area must be addressed in some kind of ongoing way to live that balanced life you seek.

This is a good section to return to on at least a yearly basis and answer these same questions again. The amount of change we are capable of is up to each one of us and no one holds you back from feeling fulfilled and happy in every area of life but you.

> *The most common way people give up their power is by thinking they don't have any.*
>
> Alice Walker

There Are Many Paths Up The Mountain. You Choose Yours.

Whenever you see a successful business, someone once made a courageous decision.

Peter Drucker

Section 5

Salon Life 101

Section 5
Salon Life 101

Many of your goals will probably be focused on your professional life. These could include professional development, career finances, perhaps even owning a salon or several salons! I had many goals early on in my career and those changed and morphed as I grew as a stylist and as a person.

It was really in listening to my clients that I came to realise that I'm so much more than a hairdresser. We don't just 'do hair' we listen to our clients through the good times and bad. We offer consolation and inspiration at times and often do a great deal of counselling. In fact, there were many days I felt I did 30% hair and 70% counselling!

When we physically touch a client, we have a much more personal connection to them. We have to touch to do our job, but that connection lowers the normal barriers people have around their emotions. When we put our hands on their shoulders, touch their hair, take them to the massage basin and massage their scalp, those communication barriers fall dramatically. This is when the client relaxes and feels the connection that we have made with them.

I have often heard it said that, "In the hairdressing industry, we have a license to touch people". I feel this is both physical and metaphorical. In this close environment we physically touch, and that touch builds a close relationship between the client and the hairdresser. This relationship grows stronger with every client visit.

Whenever you see a successful person, you only see the public glories, never the private sacrifices to reach them.

Vaibhav Shah

From regular visits, we become very familiar with our clients. We learn about one another and in no time at all, our clients are telling us the utmost personal information about themselves. They share happiness, sadness, extreme emotional pain as well as joy. The bottom line is that this is a personal relationship to the client, but it is also a business relationship. As hairdressers we must honor that knowledge in order to maintain our client base.

In this section, I will talk to you about growing a fantastic business. While it's easy to assume I would offer several 'big' ideas that will be stunningly successful, business is really about the little things. The things that seem small tend to be those things that will cost you big in the long run if ignored.

While it's easy to set aside or ignore these little things, the fact that clients have an emotional connection to their hairdresser makes it even more critical that you pay attention. For example, if you were to go into a store where no one knows you and be ignored or treated rudely by a worker in that store, it's probably not that big of a deal. You don't take it all that personally because you are more or less anonymous.

However, in a salon you must remember that people do feel connected. So, if they go into their regular salon and are ignored or treated rudely, they take it very personally. Not only may they never come back, they tell their family, their friends and their coworkers.

One of the better aspects of being in the salon business is that it is quite easy to get referrals when people love you and feel they are treated well. But that can also work against you if they are treated rudely and instead of losing one client, you may lose five or six.

I bring this up because I feel it is the number one reason that some stylists and salons fail. They don't treat their clients well and this is backed up with statistics that show 62% of people change salons because they are treated rudely. Not because of the prices, location, marketing or any of the other many things that salon owners focus on.

It is absolutely how they are treated. Perhaps they felt rushed or not heard by their stylist. Perhaps they felt treated like just a number rather than a person. Perhaps they got tired of all the negative emotion and chatter in a particular salon. Clients want to feel special and they want you to understand them as a person, not just another cut.

The environment within your salon also has to be welcoming and attentive to client needs. Clients must be greeted, smiled at, made to feel comfortable. No matter what else is going on, the client experience must be number one. Almost every single goal or desire you have as a stylist or salon owner goes back to that one thing.

Want more clients? Treat your existing clients better.

Want more referrals? Treat your existing clients better.

Want clients to stay with you for decades? Treat your existing clients better.

I think you get the idea. You must start right where you are and improve that before you can level up. You begin the level up process by adding to your skills and offering those to existing clients first. If they already love your work, it will naturally expand.

Now think about your own salon environment and try to view it as a client. How do you feel clients are treated now?

_____
_____
_____
_____
_____
_____
_____
_____
_____
_____
_____
_____
_____
_____
_____
_____

List several things you feel would improve the client experience in your salon.

_____
_____
_____
_____
_____
_____
_____
_____
_____
_____
_____
_____
_____
_____
_____
_____

You Are Fully In Charge Of YOU!

As I talked about in my book, I wanted to be the Queen of up styles. I wanted to get into the wedding and formal market. Not just because it was more lucrative, which it is, but also because I felt it was among the top skill sets I could acquire as a stylist. I knew that if I wanted that market, and those clients, I not only had to gain that skill, I also had to present myself as a consummate professional.

That started with realising my existing clients have a need for wedding or formal services too. I started with them. You don't have to 'attract' a whole new client base for a particular service, you just need to add skills your existing clients need and that others will need as well.

What skill sets would you like to add to your business? List them.

_____
_____
_____
_____
_____
_____
_____
_____
_____
_____
_____
_____
_____
_____

You also ensure that every single client is well treated from the moment they step in the salon to the moment they leave. They are greeted with a smile, welcomed and treated to a very professional environment. You dress the part of professional – no sloppy t-shirts and jeans! You act the part of professional – talk positively about other clients or hairdressers. You focus on the client by listening to them, allowing them to talk and taking the time to know them as people.

I have often had hairdressers ask me how they can attract higher level clients who will pay more. I get what they are saying, they want to increase revenue by upping prices and offering more expensive services. There is nothing wrong with that, by the way, but I really think they are looking at the equation backward. You have to work on you first and you are fully in charge of YOU!

Before you can attract higher level clients, you have to bring your skills and presentation to a higher professional level. Remember that clients are coming to you for an experience, not just a cut or color. If the experience is unprofessional or rude, you will never attract a different, or higher, clientele.

List five ways you can 'level up' and be more professional right now.

_____
_____
_____
_____
_____
_____
_____
_____
_____
_____
_____
_____
_____
_____
_____
_____

It is amazing how much you can change starting right where you are just by being more professional. As we grow as hairdressers, we understand that clients rely on us for more advice than just about hair. Of course, we are eager to recommend products they might benefit from and this can add to our business' bottom line too. But they also are interested in other beauty advice.

Everything from skin care to makeup and fashion. These are often overlooked ways to improve the relationships you have now with clients. You become their local expert on trends and products so they get the best, most current information while sitting in your chair. This isn't hard to do, but just takes a little effort on your part and better communication skills.

Now look back at the previous sections where we talked about the various personality types. Think about your various clients. Can you guess which personality type a few of them fall into? How can you use that information to communicate better with that person? Once someone sits in your chair, it is all about how you communicate, and improving those skills will improve your overall business tremendously!

Now, list several things you are going to do this week to improve communication with your clients. Be specific even listing certain clients that have been challenging.

_____
_____
_____
_____
_____
_____
_____
_____
_____
_____
_____
_____
_____
_____
_____
_____
_____
_____
_____
_____
_____

Workplace Communication

There is no doubt you will need great communication skills in the workplace. Not only for clients but for coworkers. These coworker relationships can be some of the most influential and positive of your professional life, but they can also turn quite toxic if not handled well. We can all learn to communicate better but remember that all you can control is you. However, by understanding more about the various personalities you work with, you will be better able to manage issues that will arise on occasion.

Before we get into conflict directly, it is important to understand the different types of conflict and how it manifests.

Essentially there are four basic types of conflict. They are:

1. Intra-Personal — Within the individual.

The easiest way to describe this if you can imagine someone who seems angry at the world. They are constantly mad and set off very easily. They don't like themselves and they don't like anyone else. This is a conflict within that person. There could be many sources or reasons for that conflict, but often it manifests as anger or overreaction to the issue at hand no matter how large or small.

2. Inter-Personal — Between individuals.

We are all very familiar with this type of conflict because this is usually what arises between those we work with. Often the conflict can occur because of inability to navigate personality differences or lack of mutual understanding, but none the less we have all experienced personal drama or conflict with another individual.

3. Personal/Functional — Between individual and job.

This type of conflict is basically someone who hates their job. They hate being a stylist or they may hate being a salon owner. It is interesting that many people will stay in a job that is not right for them just because they have spent so much time and money learning that job. Being a stylist is all about people and if you hate your job, you must find something else to do. There is no way to hide this conflict from your clients and it is extremely damaging.

4. Personal/Organisational – Between individual and organisation.

This type of conflict I have both experienced and witnessed. It is when someone isn't a good fit for that salon. They may not be able to get along with coworkers or they may consider the existing environment toxic, but whatever the issue it is a conflict between one person and the organisation they work for.

Now think back to the Anger Iceberg illustration. It is very common for conflict on any of these levels to manifest as anger. This is because conflict is expressed through feelings which then become behaviours such as:

- Anger – Fear
- Disappointment
- Frustration
- Hostility
- Depression
- Say hurtful things
- Inability to empathise
- Passive aggressive behaviour
- Envious of success of others

How does this happen? How can a seemingly normal workplace relationship get off track and then become toxic? If it happens, how do you fix it? Before I start with explanation of how work relationships are created or can get off track, I want you to ask yourself the following questions:

1. Is your communication productive or toxic? Do people describe you as 'difficult' and if so, in what way?

_____
_____
_____
_____
_____
_____
_____

2. Are you able to communicate about difficult topics effectively or not? Describe a specific situation.

_____
_____
_____
_____
_____
_____
_____
_____

3. Do you put off discussing subjects for fear of the outcome? Describe a time this happened.

_____
_____
_____
_____
_____
_____
_____
_____

4. Do you feel learning to communicate better with your coworkers will help you? In what way?

_____
_____
_____
_____
_____
_____
_____
_____

In order to discover how to effectively build or improve relationships in the workplace, I have created the following chart and explanation. In this chart, the right hand side is the positive side and the left hand side is the negative side:

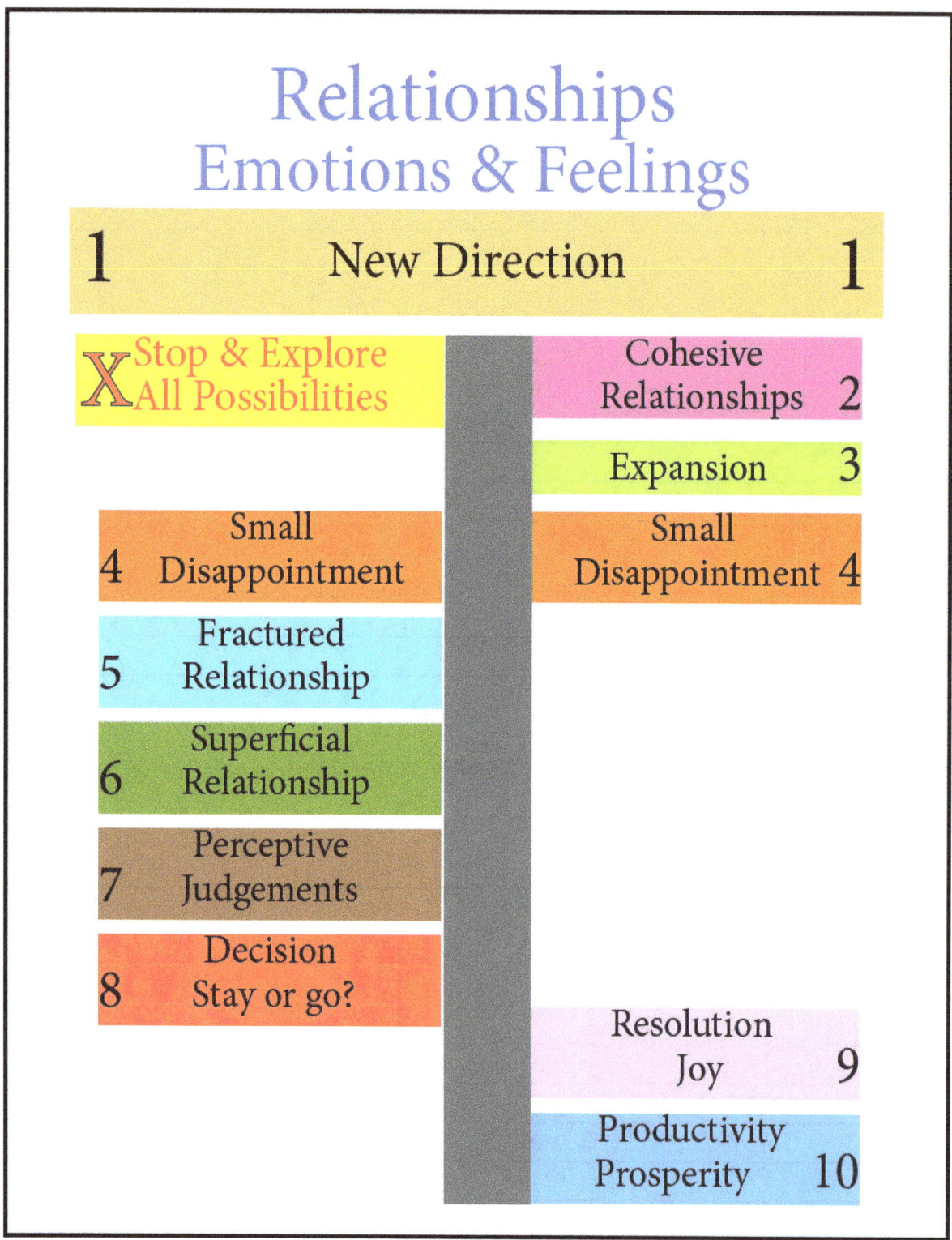

Stage One: A New Direction

This is at the beginning of your workplace experience. It is very exciting. Perhaps you are in a salon for the first time or have moved to a new salon. You are thinking about how things will go and what you can achieve. Everything is new and it is important to keep an open mind and progress slowly. You will get a lot of information during this stage and you must process it.

Everyone is on their best behaviour as you are assessing each other's personality and performance. You may feel as if you are putting on your best face and we all do this at the beginning of a new work experience or each time a new stylist joins our salon.

Stage Two: Cohesive Relationships

Relating effectively to others in the workplace begins with you knowing yourself on a mental, emotional, physical and spiritual level, while being very clear on your own values and work ethics. You are open to hearing others' ideas and willing to share your ideas and talents as a team member working in harmony.

The key to this stage of relationship is where you learn about each other's strengths and weaknesses. It is very important to have an understanding that colleagues have past hurts and painful experiences with former workers. Peoples past experiences that are hidden beneath the surface need to be dealt with otherwise they could spoil new relationships. The same is true of yourself. If you carry forward your own past hurts and negative experiences, it will impact those new relationships as well. Each person should take this stage very slowly in order to process/understand where you feel the relationships are going and how you perceive the personalities involved.

Stage Three: Expansion

This stage is when everyone is up to speed and working well. Team members are enthusiastic and totally committed. They have gained a deeper understanding of themselves and each other and how well they work together, how complementary they are, where strengths and weaknesses lie, and how to remedy those weaknesses in building a strong productive team. Energy levels are high in this stage, and members of the team are clear in their communication and emotionally honest with each other and motivated. These signs are all indicators of a healthy, productive, strong functioning team.

The members are clear on their own, and each other's, values some of these being loyalty, genuineness, sincerity, respectful of self, others and the project. Self-care is important and any hint of backbiting or unhealthy competitiveness is a destroyer of team success.

Stage Four: Small Disappointment

The fourth stage is the "MOST IMPORTANT" stage in building a healthy relationship with team members. This stage must not be ignored; it's the first "HINT" of disappointment so small it's hardly worth mentioning. In fact, you may worry that to even mention the situation could sound petty. Perhaps something as small as coming in late one day and inconveniencing your coworkers.

Now imagine swallowing down one small grape of irritation, then another grape of sadness, another of disappointment, another of not being acknowledged and pretty soon you end up with a big belly full of sour, unresolved grapes. Imagine that one day, usually over something very small, out of nowhere spews a belly full of exploding anger (sour grapes that have built up and gone rotten).

You become very angry at everyone and everything. Team members then may begin questioning and wonder if you have gone crazy. What was that all about?

Another common destructive behaviour is backbiting, where a team member feels they just have to vent to another member and get the issue off their chest, rather than speaking to the person that they have the issue with. This behaviour can cause untold long-term damage to that specific relationship but also to the entire team as well because trust is lost.

You will notice that 'small disappointment' is on both sides of the chart. This is because if it is addressed with sincerity straight away, and resolved, the relationships can move on to stage 9. If it is not addressed, it will track along the negative side until resolved.

Stage 5: Fractured Relationship

By overlooking those seemingly small issues, or leaving them unresolved, the team is weakened. Once that occurs, team members often withdraw from each other. This is where passive aggressive behaviours can be born; the team stagnates and begins to focus on the negative.

As I've said many times, what we focus on expands and that includes negativity. The team becomes fragmented; each member rowing their own boat. Trust is lost, members of the team start to build scenarios and form perceptions about what each other may be thinking which are untrue. Stress runs rampant due to the unresolved conflict and resulting behaviours.

Now begins a rapid decline. Relationships have broken down, communication is lost, feelings of betrayal, abandonment, resentment and other negative thoughts and feelings grow. Backbiting and negative energy infiltrates every part of the salon. You can be amazed at how quickly this can happen. A salon can devolve from a well-functioning and productive team to chaos in a very short period of time.

Stage 6: Superficial Relationship

In this stage, the fear of disappointment and betrayal (stages 4 and 5), have not been addressed. Therefore, the relationship has superficially adjusted itself - in other words, it has become fake and insincere. There is an uneasiness overshadowing the relationship.

Team members begin building emotional walls to protect themselves, not realising that these walls further separate them from the team. The longer this goes on, the higher and thicker these walls become between team members.

Blame is the wedge used to drive team members farther apart. Behind closed doors bitterness, anger and resentment build up, however they show the public the fake appearance that "all is well in my world".

Stage 7: Perceptive Judgments

The wedge has been driven in so deeply that the relationships have now become stagnant. The emotions are out of balance and the indication is that some deep disappointment or betrayal has still not been resolved. They each start to evaluate all the negative issues of team members rather than the positive. They tear each other down and credibility may be lost between the team members.

Backbiting escalates even more, in the name of venting, and this is the most destructive behaviour of all as those words can never be taken back fully. This illustrates how important it is not to escalate issues or keep them inside as it can do irreparable damage.

Stage 8: Decision: Stay or go?

This stage is make or break. You either find the courage to go back and resolve the first hint of disappointment or you must leave. There is still the possibility to get back on track positively after resolving this crisis, but only by facing the issues head on and resolving them. If this is finally done, the team grows stronger and gains the lessons learned through the tough times. They all discover that finding a resolution sooner, rather than later, is better with even the smallest conflict. They now actively choose not to escalate.

Some people find confronting a situation very challenging and scary and they may choose to leave rather than learn the hard lessons. When people make the choice to leave and are still unresolved, they will often recreate a similar situation in their new position or in their private lives. This cycle can continue until a decision is made to resolve the original issue. Some people hang onto old hurts and make the choice to never deal with issues. These people often blame others rather than take personal responsibility.

The most obvious sign of this type of 'serial unresolver' is the length of time they stay at a salon (or in a personal relationship). If they can't make it past two years at any of their previous jobs, then odds are they don't have the skills to manage conflict or work effectively in a team environment. They have decided it is easier to leave rather than go through something difficult.

Stage 9: Resolution/Joy

Once the conflict is resolved, the relationship is deepened. The person who was hurt feels heard and validated by expressing their feelings of disappointment. Apologies are made, discussion is had about the lesson learned while harmony and balance is restored in the team. The relationships and trust now move to a much deeper level through the gentle voice of emotional honesty and shared lessons learned.

Stage 10: Productivity/Prosperity

The transformation is complete, harmony and peace has been restored to the team, the members have a deeper understanding of each other and a stronger awareness of boundaries and respect for both the team and individuals.

This cycle will appear in varying intensity each and every time a new person is added to the mix or even when one leaves the team. Work relationships are quite complex and new personalities, or issues with those who are not known as well, can create tremendous upheaval if not handled immediately and effectively.

The lesson or take away for you here is that dealing with the small things will have big reward and alleviate much stress in your life.

Now think back to a time when you joined a work situation or had a conflict with a new team member. Describe what happened:

_____
_____
_____
_____
_____
_____
_____
_____
_____
_____
_____

How do you feel this might have been resolved if you'd understood then, what you know now about how teams work together?

_____
_____
_____
_____
_____
_____
_____
_____

Workplace Conflict Ladder

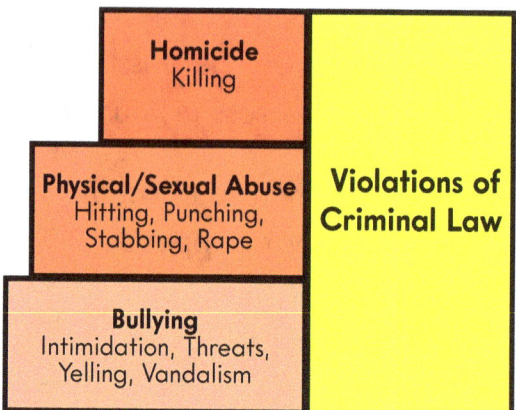

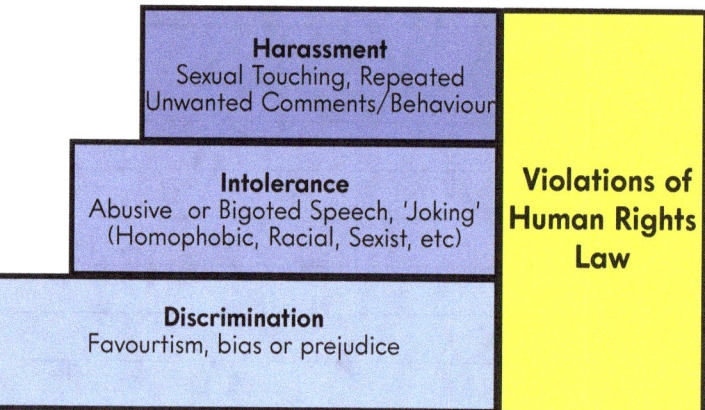

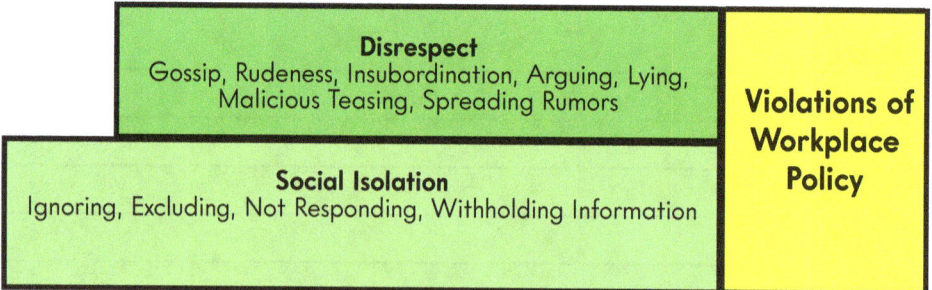

A Respectful Workplace
has well defined policies and procedures, open communication, embraces diversity,
is collaborative and inclusive.

This diagram shows a workplace conflict ladder. It categorises the escalation of conflict in accordance with their legal descriptions. It is important to note that Bullying is categorised with Violations of Criminal Law. Bullying is one of the most common types of workplace conflict that most people encounter and few realise that the consequences for that behavior extend far beyond simple personal interaction and can have legal implications for both the employee and employer.

A worker is considered to be bullied at work if a person, or group of people, repeatedly act 'unreasonably' towards them or a group of workers. Bullying can also mean any behaviour that creates a risk to health and safety. Unreasonable behaviour includes actions such as victimising, humiliating, intimidating or threatening.

Examples of bullying include:

- **Behaving aggressively**
- **Teasing or practical jokes**
- **Pressuring someone to behave inappropriately**
- **Excluding someone from work-related events**
- **Unreasonable work demands**

Workplace conflict and bully behaviours is bad for business because it can lead to downturns in productivity and increases in absenteeism.

Impacts of Bullying on the Individual

Workplace bullying can affect people in a number of ways, resulting in:

- **Distress, anxiety, panic attacks or sleep disturbance**
- **Physical illness, such as muscular tension, headaches and digestive problems**
- **Reduced work performance**
- **Loss of self-esteem and feelings of isolation**
- **Deteriorating relationships with colleagues, family and friends**
- **Depression**
- **Increased risk of suicide**

The diagram on the next page shows a quick visual of the impacts and result bullying and other conflict can have if not addressed in a nonviolent way. For those that are bullied, it can result in depression, anxiety or a combination of both.

As shown in the illustration, depression is a result of living in the past. This includes worry over things that already happened that cannot be changed and stress from carrying around old hurts and failures. This illustration shows the depression cycle and how it can run in a continuous loop, intensifying when there is conflict in relationships.

The lower portion of the illustration shows a similar result when one focuses on fear of the future. Anxiety is the result of worrying about all the 'what ifs' and expecting the worst. While it has a similar loop as depression, it can have a tremendous effect on the physical wellbeing of the person.

Anxiety is a combination of behavioural, physiological and cognitive factors. The idea of what 'might' happen produces physiological symptoms such as palpitations, constant tension, headaches, inability to sleep and many others. Once these symptoms appear, the cognitive reactive thoughts emerge. These thoughts focus on the fear and inability to control your emotions. The thoughts worry about what others think and that their panic many be obvious to those around them.

These physiological symptoms and reactive thoughts combine to produce an increase in overall anxiety. This increase levels up the cognitive issues with fearful thoughts of anticipation of the worst. Fears such as "I won't sleep" or "I will panic" can actually bring those fears into being. This produces the behavioural issue of avoidance and chronic anxiety.

Many people who experience one, or both, of these issues struggle with them long term if the source of conflict is never addressed. If good communication and conflict management skills are not learned, they can be devastating mentally and physically.

Many of the communication skills I talk about in my book and this workbook focus on the present - the here and now. This is why the circle of control is so important as it focuses your attention on what you have control over right now, today. It allows you to take action and improve your skills to break free from these terrible cycles and reduce the conflict in every relationship in your life.

Past

Depression
Living in the Past

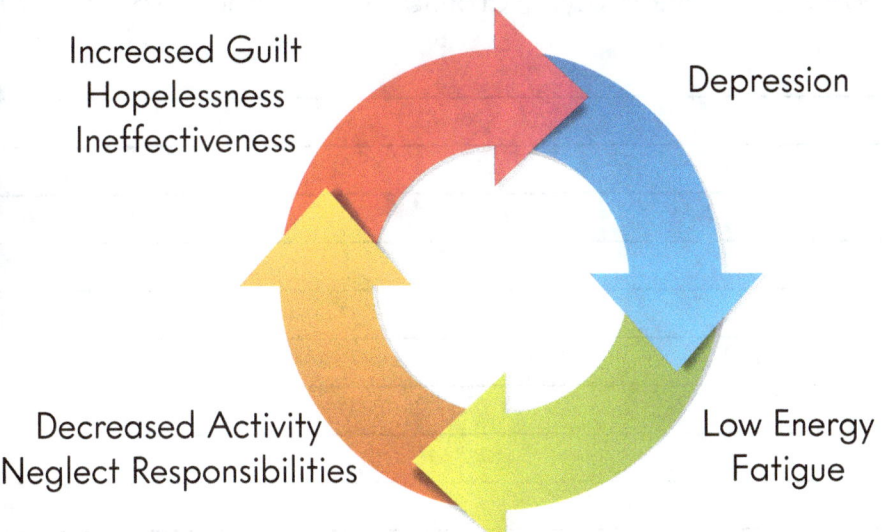

Increased Guilt
Hopelessness
Ineffectiveness

Depression

Low Energy
Fatigue

Decreased Activity
Neglect Responsibilities

Present - Now

Anxiety
Fear of the Future

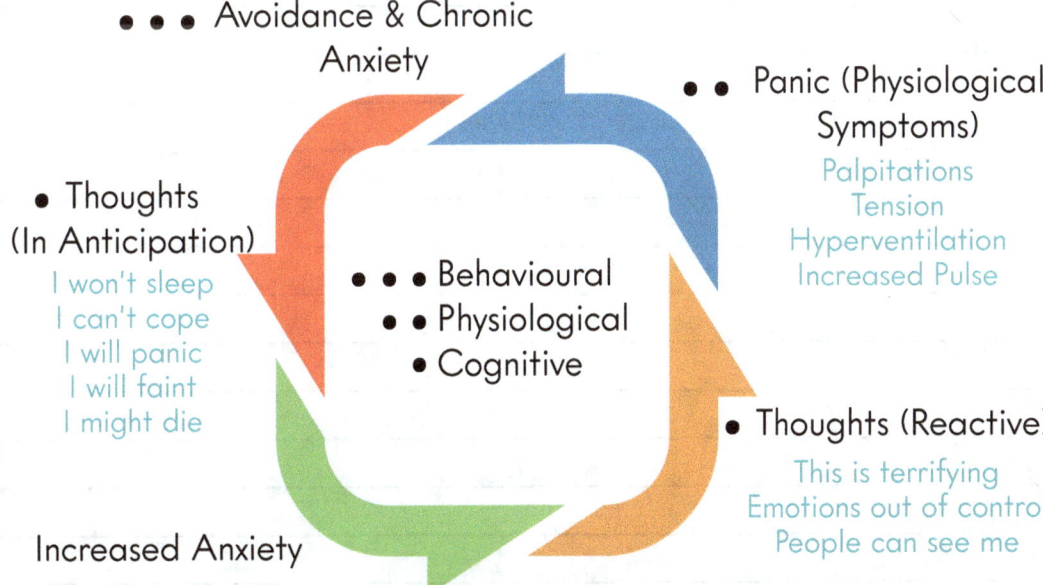

• • • Avoidance & Chronic Anxiety

• • Panic (Physiological Symptoms)
Palpitations
Tension
Hyperventilation
Increased Pulse

• Thoughts (In Anticipation)
I won't sleep
I can't cope
I will panic
I will faint
I might die

• • • Behavioural
• • Physiological
• Cognitive

• Thoughts (Reactive)
This is terrifying
Emotions out of control
People can see me

Increased Anxiety

Future

Issues of Bullying will arise on occasion and the best way to prepare is to think through how you will respond rather than just reacting in the moment. Answer the following questions and think through your possible responses.

Does your workplace have a policy around bullying and if so what it is?

_____
_____
_____
_____
_____
_____
_____
_____
_____
_____
_____
_____
_____

How would you change or improve bullying awareness in your current workplace?

_____
_____
_____
_____
_____
_____
_____
_____
_____
_____
_____
_____
_____
_____

Have you ever been involved in an incident of workplace bullying. Describe how it made you feel:

___

If you witnessed, or were the victim of, bullying in the workplace, how would you deal with it?

___

I can't change the direction of the wind, but I can adjust my sails to always reach my destination.

Jimmy Dean

Section 6

Taming Life's Split Ends

Section 6
Taming Life's Split Ends

There are times in each person's life when we feel frazzled, stressed and are just trying to hold it together and get through each day. However, if that type of stress goes on too long it can have devastating long-term effects. Your life will feel out of control, unruly and fractured.

Few people realise that stress is cumulative and over time each stressor builds upon the next creating a storm of anger and frustration within you. One of the best things you can ever do for yourself as you set out to achieve your goals, is to implement the idea of peace in your life.

Now I'm not saying that every single day will be nothing but peace, far from it. But if you mindfully approach each day with the intent on interjecting peace in as many ways as possible, then over time it happens. In small ways at first, but after a while you will find you are happier. Not necessarily because everything is perfect in your life, but because you know you are paying attention to those things that are important to you – and delegating or deleting everything else.

This idea of a peaceful life is really what is behind the current 'minimalism' movement that has swept the world. It suggests that by decluttering your life and worrying less about 'things' you make room for what is important, and you gain a great deal of peace. It's true on every level but especially when it comes to time management and conflict.

Remember when you were setting goals, I talked about the fact that you can easily get rid of at least ten percent of the tasks that take your time now. You do this by delegating those tasks to others, combining the tasks together or deleting the tasks altogether.

It is important to think about what is really valuable in your life and the most valuable thing you have is your time.

Ask yourself, how do you want to spend that time and who do you want to spend it with?

_____
_____
_____
_____
_____
_____
_____
_____
_____
_____

When you look at the tasks you have to do today or this week, ask yourself, will this matter in five years? Take a long view of your life and don't waste time on tasks that suck the life out of you.

Hard Conversations

The most difficult aspect of anyone's life is having hard conversations. This could be with family or coworkers or anyone. If you really want to change, and you commit to reach your goals, it will probably entail having some difficult conversations. When you want to achieve that peace in your life that we all crave, it may mean confronting some old conflicts or apologising to some people to clear the air. It may mean choosing to talk about difficult subjects in better ways than you have in the past.

None of these things are easy. They are more difficult if you don't have good communication skills. I was in a workshop one day with a team from a salon in a neighboring town. As we discussed the ideas of resolving conflict one question kept coming up repeatedly: "How?"

I explained the ideas again only to end with some participants asking the same question, "How?" I realised that several of these team members were young and this was really their first exposure to the ideas of workplace or team culture.

Others were much older and clearly had a set pattern of trying to resolve conflict that wasn't working for them. A few of them also talked about their personal relationships and what a struggle they were.

I realised it is not enough to tell someone to sit and have a 'conversation'. They needed a very clear road map. A game plan they could think about at length before meeting with that person so they would feel prepared. They needed to know how to disagree without it becoming a shouting match. They needed to know how to manage conflict if there is no resolution.

While I can't tell someone word for word what to say during a hard conversation, I can give you some very specific tools and techniques that will work in almost any situation. I am including the information in this workbook because no matter your age or place in life, we can all manage conflict better.

When you must have a difficult conversation with someone, no matter if they are a coworker or family member, the same ideas still apply. First, you must think about how to approach the subject and that is best addressed with the acronym CALM.

Successful and unsuccessful people do not vary greatly in their abilities. They vary in their desires to reach their potential.

John Maxwell

CALM

C – Clarify: Identify the issue or issues and think about how you would like to be approached before approaching the other person. When meeting together, focus on the issue not emotion. Leave the past, or any previous disagreements, out of the current conversation. Think the issue through and remove as much of your own emotion as possible. Write out in a notebook what you would like to say and make it as professional as possible without accusations or personal attacks.

A – Address: Ask that person to meet with you. Set a specific time to talk with the person(s) involved and choose a place that is quiet and non-threating. For example, if you want to speak with a coworker you might ask them to coffee or meet somewhere other than the salon. You want to avoid interruptions and distractions. If you want to discuss something like finances with your partner, ask a friend or family member to take the kids and have a quiet conversation at the kitchen table with all the information at hand.

L – Listen: Really listen to the other person's perspective and try to understand their point of view. Don't interrupt or defend your position. Repeat back to them what you thought they said to be sure you understand them and they know you are listening. For example, "If I understood correctly, you are saying that the noise from my workstation is distracting and makes it hard for you to speak to your clients and be heard. Is that correct?"

M – Manage: Discuss ideas for possible steps to take and expected outcomes. Create a 'next steps' to do list for each of you. It is never just one person's issue or problem. Take responsibility for your part in the issue and be sincere. Part of this step should also include a commitment to talk frequently about any small issues, so they don't become big issues. The natural response to conflict is to withdraw, but the cure is to communicate more, so make that part of the next steps.

Maintaining Respect

The next part of having a difficult conversation is the ability to maintain respect even if you disagree. This is often where so many people get off track. They become emotional about the issue, the conversation devolves into name calling and anger then the problem is worse than it was before.

Most would say that the possibility of a conversation devolving into an emotional mess is the main reason they avoid hard conversations like the plague. Nothing scares another human more than hearing the words "We need to talk."

I have developed a short list of tips to help remove that fear. It takes some practice but as with anything, the more you engage with people in a respectful manner the easier it gets. How you phrase your ideas and comments is key to remaining respectful.

6 Respectful Disagreement Tips

- **Keep conversation focused on task or issue and avoid personal attacks:** "Can you walk me through your thought process for this request?" vs. "Why would you think this was a good idea?"

- **Avoid using general phrases:** "You always" or "You Never".

- **Check for understanding and avoid assumptions.** "Can you give me some detail on your request? I don't mind helping but have two deadlines this week." vs. "Why would you ask me to help? Don't you know how busy I am?"

- **Keep tone pleasant and voices lowered.**

- **If things get too heated or emotional, simply say:** "Why don't we revisit this when we have had some time to think about it?" Deescalate quickly and step away if need be.

- **Accept what you can't change or is out of your control and then let it go.** You can only control you and carrying anger around hurts you in the long run.

I will absolutely acknowledge that there are times when there is no resolution and you must agree to disagree. This is the only way to let it go and move beyond the issue especially when you still have to work with that person. However, like most things involving conflict that is easier said than done. How do you really let it go?

Perhaps you have that one coworker who you can't resolve anything with or perhaps you have a family member that won't let you leave things in the past. What then? Remember that the only person you can improve is you.

There comes a time you must accept that others may not want to change at all and that is their choice. You don't have to allow it to continue to affect your life negatively. Below are a few tips on managing conflict when there is no resolution.

- **Understand your own natural behaviours and work on your shortcomings. Know your personality type and work on understanding others better.**

- **Accept responsibility for mistakes/behaviours and fix or change them so future relationships will be better.**

- **Before you speak, stop and think how your words will be perceived. Many disagreements occur because of attitude and tone rather than what is actually said.**

- **When someone speaks to you, respond-don't react. Stop and think before you say anything.**

- **If a situation/interaction is causing conflict, communicate more not less. Be open about the small things and clear things up quickly. Don't stop communicating.**

- **Understand that you will not always like the people you deal with, but you MUST develop a professional understanding and respect in order to work together. This shows your professionalism and ability to work as a team member. Remove the ego from the equation and things will go much smoother.**

- **Do not take your grievance to the masses (negative talk/manipulate) as it only builds conflict and can cause hard feelings to linger. Once you become the person who talks about others, no one will have trust or respect for you. Be the person others can trust in and all your relationships will improve.**

Now think back to the last conflict or hard conversation you had with a coworker or family member. What happened?

_____
_____
_____
_____
_____
_____
_____
_____
_____
_____
_____
_____
_____

When you think about how that conversation evolved, what role did emotion play?

_____
_____
_____
_____
_____
_____
_____
_____
_____
_____
_____
_____
_____
_____

Think about the CALM steps. How would using those have improved that conversation?

_____
_____
_____
_____
_____
_____
_____
_____
_____
_____
_____
_____
_____
_____

Gratitude is Life Altering

Along with the book and this workbook, I have also developed a Gratitude Journal. This journal is designed for you to start each day writing those things you are grateful for and continuing through the entire year.

Gratitude is an interesting concept. It has been proven that the emotion of gratitude has a powerful effect on rewiring your subconscious mind. The feelings it promotes activate essential pleasure areas of the brain and the more you engage in gratitude, the more your brain desires that feeling. This helps tremendously especially if you have been negative in the past or are currently dealing with some negative circumstances. Even if things are going well, acknowledging gratitude in your life is very fulfilling.

Beyond the pleasure it gives to remind yourself of those events and people you are most grateful for in your life, it also sets the tone of each day. It starts you on the way to a state of peaceful mindfulness which is the ultimate goal. No matter how your day evolves, or what may transpire, you feel much more positively about it if you start with a grateful heart.

To get you started thinking with a mindset of gratitude, I want you to make a list of the 5 people in your life that you are most grateful for today and beside each one, write why.

_____
_____
_____
_____
_____
_____
_____
_____
_____
_____
_____
_____
_____

This is just a start, but I encourage you to keep a daily gratitude journal and experience the difference it will make in your overall outlook. Focused gratitude will help you reach your goals while finding the peace and joy we all want to experience.

Gaining Clarity

One of the reasons people get so overwhelmed on this journey of personal growth is because they don't know where to start and then they don't know how to make decisions once they begin. It is very common to feel that there are so many things that need attention, you become paralysed.

An important activity that helps me tremendously when I am turning over decisions in my mind or seeking clarity to deal with a difficult situation, is to declutter my surroundings. It doesn't matter if it is a work area, office or home, your immediate environment can both add to, or distract from, your sense of calm. Decluttering your home helps you to have more clarity and focus which allows you to organise your thoughts while you are getting rid of things you no longer need.

I use a very simple series of questions when I am decluttering and they may work for you as well. When clearing out clothes, cupboards, rooms, storage, with each item, ask yourself:

- Do I love it?
- Do I use it? If so, when did I use it last?
- Do I want this item in my life going forward?
- Do I have another one of these?
- Do I have something else that could serve the same purpose?
- Did I even remember I owned this?
- Would I miss it if it were gone?
- Why have I been keeping this?
- Does this item fit my current lifestyle?
- Does this fit with my goals?

My belief is that a cluttered environment produces a cluttered mind. You probably feel this same way because once your home or area is cleaned, it immediately gives you a lighter feeling. Most people don't realise that clutter creates a heavy feeling as if your life is unorganised and out of control.

Decluttering may seem a very simple technique, but it has positive effects on our mental health and mental clarity. There may be other things, even some very simple things that may be holding you back from moving toward your goals.

Ask yourself: What can I do right now to start moving on the path toward my goals? List three actions you can take tomorrow to clear your mind and get started.

_____
_____
_____
_____
_____
_____
_____
_____

Roadblock Mastermind

Each of us occasionally encounters roadblocks especially when we are striving for great things. In the book, I talked a little about how helpful mastermind groups are. These are made up of like-minded people who are striving to improve their own lives. While they may not all be hairdressers, they certainly can be.

Finding some kind of peer group that has the same drive and intentions as you do is extremely important. I have heard it said by many successful people that you will have the same level of success as the five people you spend the most time around. Mastermind groups are full of people who want more success than they have experienced before, and they need that same peer support.

You may be in a similar situation. If those around you are complacent, negative, or just happy with the status quo and you aren't, then it is important to join this type of group.

This will enable you to get the support you need to get past roadblocks or overcome setbacks. It also allows you the freedom to discuss ideas that others in your life might shoot down as 'unrealistic' or 'too high level'. We all need a safe space to grow beyond who we currently are, but if all you hear is how you should be satisfied with less, and quit trying so hard to be better, it can be very discouraging.

I have participated in various mastermind groups over the years and I also run one to mentor others as well. I love being involved because it is so wonderful to hear positive people, who want to grow and change, discuss how excited they are. Even when they have a failure, the group is there for them, offering support and suggestions to get back up and try again.

There will always be roadblocks, but life is about moving past them, not focusing on the negative. I also coach people who want to improve their lives and relationships. By improving their communication skill set they are able to move farther, faster than they could ever imagine.

Now think about your life. If you had a coach or mentor in front of you right now, what questions would you ask? What would you want them to help you achieve? Make a list here:

_____
_____
_____
_____
_____
_____
_____
_____
_____
_____
_____

You can and will achieve great things if you commit to reaching the goals you have laid out for yourself. No matter what happens today, we each get to do it over again tomorrow and that is very good news indeed. Don't wait to put your plan into action. Start today and if I can help you on your journey, please contact me here:

www.donnapiromalli.com
www.griffithcounselling.com

We may encounter many defeats but we must not be defeated.

Maya Angelou

www.ingramcontent.com/pod-product-compliance
Lightning Source LLC
Chambersburg PA
CBHW081459070526
44586CB00019B/2428